DEC **1** 9 2009

sea Turtles

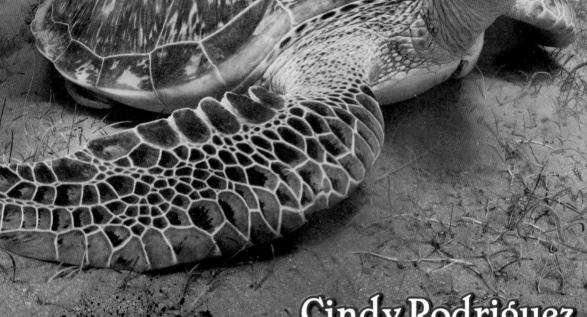

Cindy Rodriguez

EYE to EYE
with Endangered Species

ROURKE PUBLISHING
Vero Beach, Florida 32964

www.rourkepublishing.com

PHOTO CREDITS: © dejan750: Title Page; © DaveBluck: 3; © strmko: 2, 3, 12, 13; © rontography: 4; © red_moon_rise: 5; © dsabo: 4, 5; © Tammy616: 6, 7, 14, 15; © eva serrabassa: 6; © YinYang: 7; © Maxhomand: 7; © scatterly: 7; © tswinner: 7; © Lynn Stone: 8, 9; © JacobH: 8, 9; © andipantz: 10; © RapidEye: 10, 11; © Fish and Wildlife Service: 11, 21; © DJMattaar: 12; © Wildlife Computers: 13; © Naluphoto: 14; © flyingdouglas: 15; © diephosi: 15; © johnandersonphoto: 16, 17; © Shutterstock: 16; © Wikipedia: 18; © dsafanda: 18, 19; © NoDerog: 19; © SecondShot: 20; © Emre YILDIZ: 20, 21; © simongurney: 22; © Kristian Sekulic: 23; © triggerfishsoul: 24

Editor: Jeanne Sturm
Cover design by Teri Intzegian
Page design by Renee Brady

Library of Congress Cataloging-in-Publication Data

Rodriguez, Cindy.
  Sea turtles / Cindy Rodriguez.
      p. cm. -- (Eye to eye with endangered species)
  Includes index.
  ISBN 978-1-60694-405-9 (hard cover)
  ISBN 978-1-60694-844-6 (soft cover)
  1. Sea turtles--Juvenile literature. I. Title.
  QL666.C536R64 2010
  597.92'8--dc22

                        2009005996

Printed in the USA

CG/CG

ROURKE PUBLISHING

www.rourkepublishing.com - rourke@rourkepublishing.com
Post Office Box 643328 Vero Beach, Florida 32964

Table of Contents

Meet the Sea Turtle

Sea turtles have survived for more than 110 million years. With all that history behind them, it's surprising how little we know about them.

One thing we do know is there are seven species of sea turtles. They are the green sea turtle, loggerhead, Kemp's ridley, olive ridley, hawksbill, flatback, and leatherback.

Hawksbill

Loggerhead

Total population counts are unknown because male and baby sea turtles do not come on shore. This mystery actually aids in their survival. As biologists study sea turtles, they learn about some of the threats to the **endangered** animals and work to find solutions.

Fun Fact

*Endangered means any species in danger of **extinction**, or disappearing completely.*

Yummy Meals!

The sea turtle's jaw determines its diet. Green turtles are **herbivorous**. Their serrated jaws helps them eat a vegetarian diet of sea grasses and algae. The **carnivorous** hawksbill has a beak-like jaw that lets it feed on meats such as sponges, shrimp, and squid found in coral reefs.

Squid

Kelp and Algae

Jellyfish

The large jaws of the loggerhead and ridley are made for crushing and grinding. They are **omnivorous**, eating both plants and meat such as crabs, shrimp, and jellyfish. Leatherback's delicate jaw must only consume soft-bodied animals.

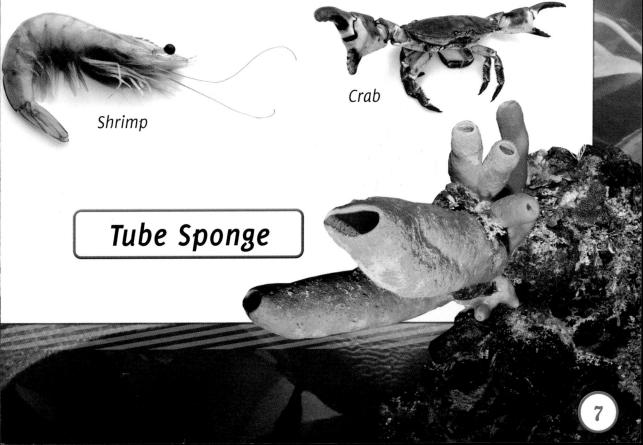

Shrimp

Crab

Tube Sponge

Nurturing the Nest

During the warmest months of the year, the female sea turtle comes ashore at night to build nests and lay her eggs.

The sea turtle uses her front and hind flippers to dig a body cavity and an egg pit for her 50 to 200 ping-pong ball size eggs. She will lay one to nine clutches or groups of eggs each season.

Loggerhead Nesting

The sand now protects the eggs from **predators**. Burying the eggs also keeps them moist and regulates their temperature.

Each step is critical to the species' survival.

The female sea turtle comes ashore to nest during high tide.

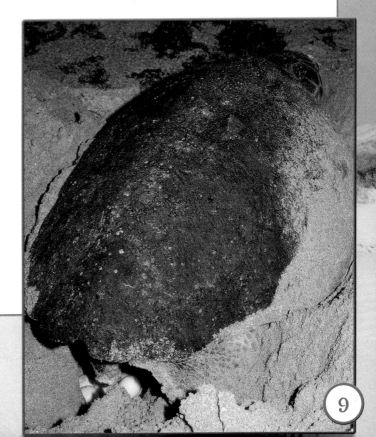

Fun Fact

Every two to three years the female sea turtle returns to her beach of origin.

Welcome, Hatchlings!

Hatchlings use a temporary egg tooth called a carbuncle to help tear open the shell. It may take these baby sea turtles three to seven days to dig their way to the surface.

Leatherback Hatchlings

The Southeast Fisheries Science Center helps conservation efforts by collecting important data on nesting behavior at this sea turtle corral in Rancho Nuevo, Mexico.

Then, at night, the hatchlings emerge from their safe underground nests. As the darkness protects them from daytime predators, the babies stay in groups moving toward the brighter light of the ocean. The hatchlings ride the **undertow** out to sea where they rest in seaweed and find their food.

Scientists estimate only one in 1,000 hatchlings will survive to become an adult sea turtle.

Sea Turtle Habitats

Sea turtles live in shallow bays, estuaries, and the open sea.

Their **migration** habits also vary; some feed and nest in the same general area, and some travel great distances between feeding and nesting.

Green turtles find food and protection on the coral reef.

Fish attach themselves to a sea turtle for protection and a free ride.

Fish

In the past, scientists tracked migration patterns using metal tags placed on the sea turtles' front flippers. Now satellites follow these movements.

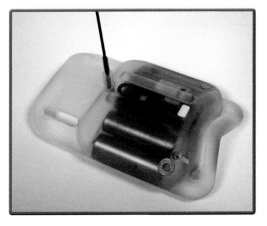

This Mk10-A tag, designed and manufactured by Wildlife Computers, collects and records data on the swimming behavior of marine animals, then transmits the information to scientists.

Danger! Sea Turtle's Enemies

Sea turtles have few natural enemies. Their biggest enemy is the careless actions of humans.

Tiger sharks eat turtles in the ocean. Hurricanes destroy thousands of their nests. Turtles must be wary of fishermen's nets and lines, and trash that could be mistaken for food. Leatherbacks might mistake plastic for a jellyfish, eat it, and die of a clogged intestine.

Tiger Shark

Fun Fact

*Green sea turtles can also get **fibropapillomas** on their skin. These tumor-like growths affect their swimming and feeding.*

Seagulls can snatch sea turtle eggs and hatchlings.

On land, **poachers**, beach developers, and predators cause difficulties for sea turtles. People illegally hunt sea turtles to eat their eggs and meat, and use their shells for combs and eyeglass frames. Fish, dogs, and seabirds eat the eggs and hatchlings. Beach development disturbs nests and confuses hatchlings trying to reach the ocean.

Help Is On the Way

Many forces are working to help the sea turtle survive its enemies. The Endangered Species Act of 1973 gives protection to the sea turtle by making it illegal to harm or disturb a sea turtle or its egg.

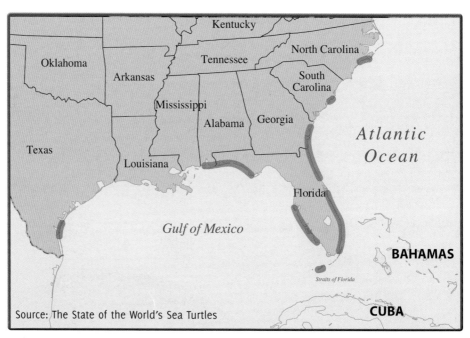

Source: The State of the World's Sea Turtles

The areas in red represent regions in the southeastern United States that are nesting areas for sea turtles. In the western U.S. sea turtle nesting areas are found along the coast of Hawaii and California.

Green Sea Turtle

17

The Turtle Excluder Device (TED) developed by the National Marine Fisheries Service is one way we can save the sea turtle. The TED is a small, metal trapdoor placed inside shrimp nets that enables the sea turtle to swim out safely before becoming tangled in the net.

The TED is 97 percent effective in helping sea turtles escape from shrimp trawls, allowing them to return to the surface to breathe.

A federally-approved habitat conservation plan protects the loggerhead turtle as it comes to nest on the east coast of Florida, one of its important nesting sites.

Biologists also help sea turtles by protecting their nests with screens or relocating them to safer areas. Some communities use special lights to avoid confusing the hatchlings.

Wildlife refuges help keep the sea turtles safe. Zoological parks like Sea World and Busch Gardens help us learn about sea turtles and how people affect their survival. These parks can protect the sea turtle's habitat, eggs, and hatchlings while studying their behavior. These zoos also offer rescue and **rehabilitation** assistance for sea turtles.

The sea turtle's powerful front flippers act like paddles. Its hind flippers serve as rudders, steering it through the water.

Researchers attach a tracking device to a turtle and release it back into the sea. The device will provide information about the animal's migration patterns and feeding habitats.

Hopefully, the actions we take today will ensure the sea turtle's future for another million years!

Glossary

biologists (bye-OL-uh-jists): scientists who study living things

carnivorous (kar-NIV-ur-uhss): animals that eat only meat

endangered (en-DAYN-jurd): when a species of plant or animal is in danger of becoming extinct, or dying out

extinction (ek-STINGKT-shuhn): when a species of plant or animal dies out

fibropapillomas (fye-broh-pa-pi-LOH-muhz): tumor-like growths

herbivorous (hur-BIV-uhr-uhss): animals that eat only plants

migration (mye-GRAY-shuhn): when a group of animals moves from one region or climate to another

omnivorous (om-NIV-ur-uhss): animals that eat both plants and meat

poachers (POHCH-urz): people who hunt illegally on land they do not own

predators (PRED-uh-turz): animals that survive by hunting other animals for food

rehabilitation (ri-huh-bil-uh-TAY-shuhn): the process of bringing an animal back to a healthy condition

undertow (UHN-dur-toh): a strong current beneath the water that pulls away from the shore

wildlife refuges (WILDE-life REF-yooj-iz): places that protect animals from danger

Index

Websites to Visit

www.turtles.org/library.htm
www.seaworld.org/infobooks/seaturtle/home.html
www.turtles.org/why.htm

About the Author

Cindy Rodriguez has been teaching first graders how to read for more than 20 years. She loves using nonfiction books to involve her students in real world situations that make their reading exciting. "Caretakers of the Earth" is the motto for Cindy's school in Vero Beach, Florida, so investigating endangered species is one of her passions. She enjoys long distance running and traveling to explore new places with her two teenage daughters.